You're a Hokie Now!

for Hokies past, present, and future

Written by Miriam Rich
Illustrated by Jonathan Kolodner

You're a Hokie now, my friend—I'm awfully proud of you.
You've walked at graduation, now there's not much left to do

But take one last look around and think of all the times we had—

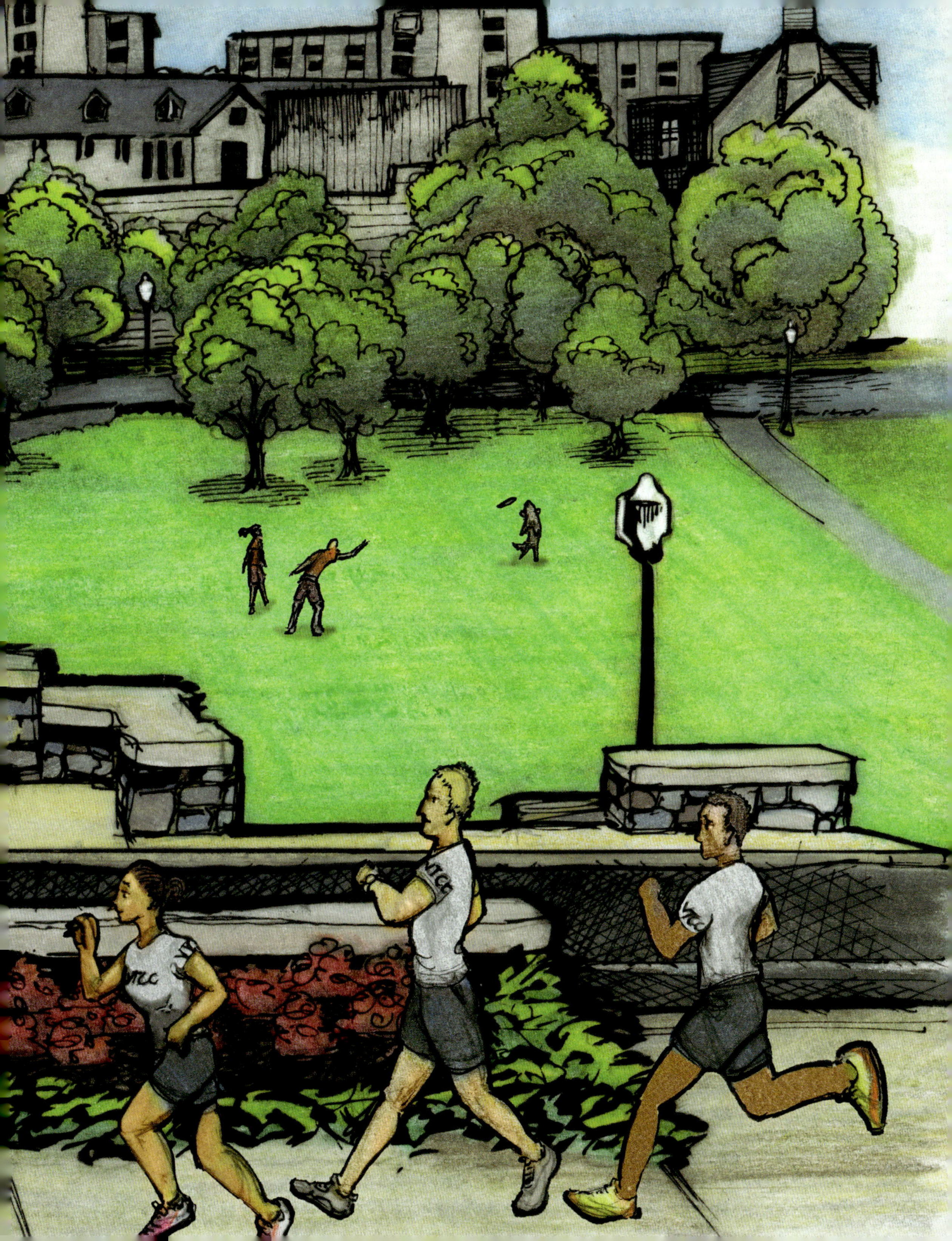

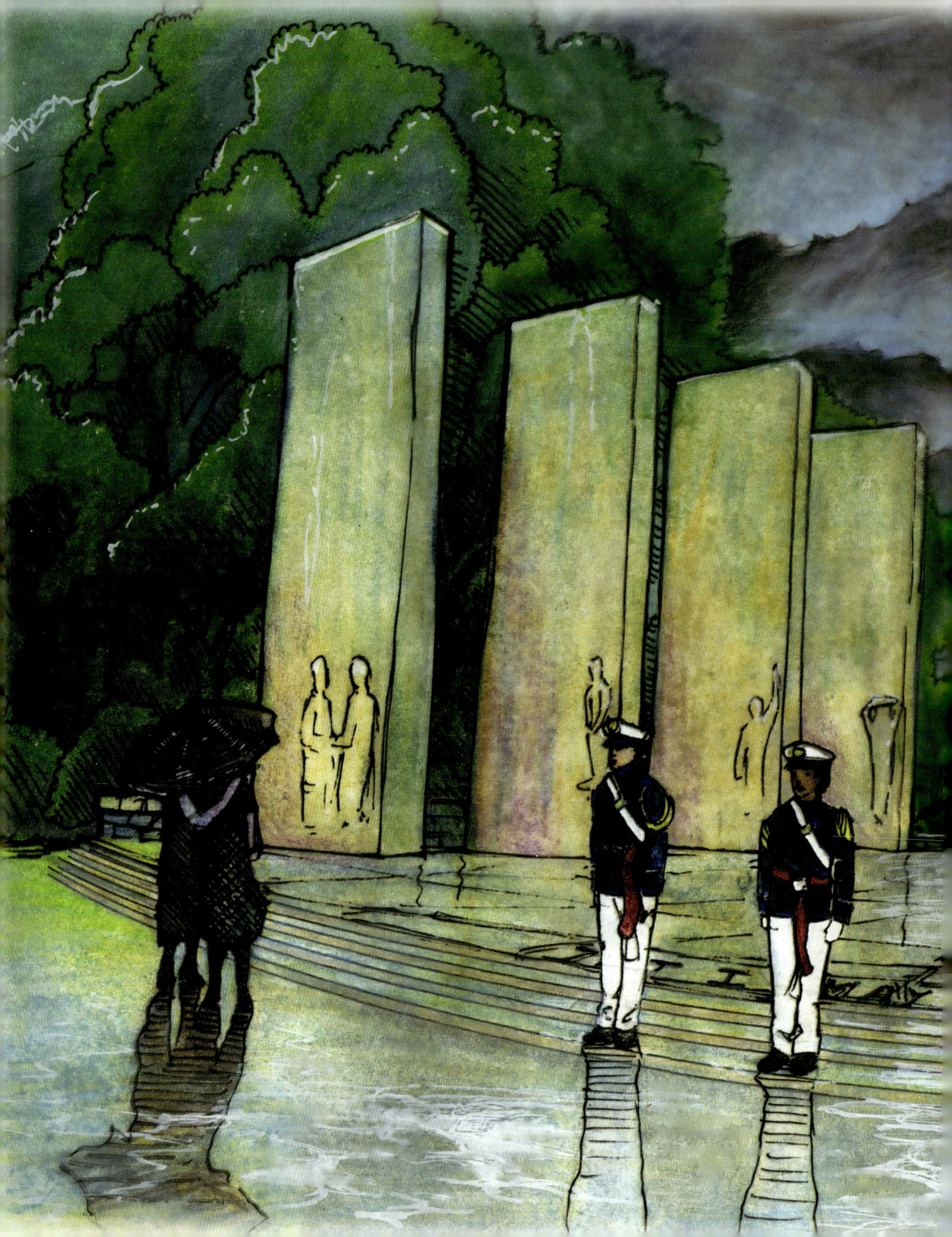

The good, the great, the really great—and yes, the very sad.

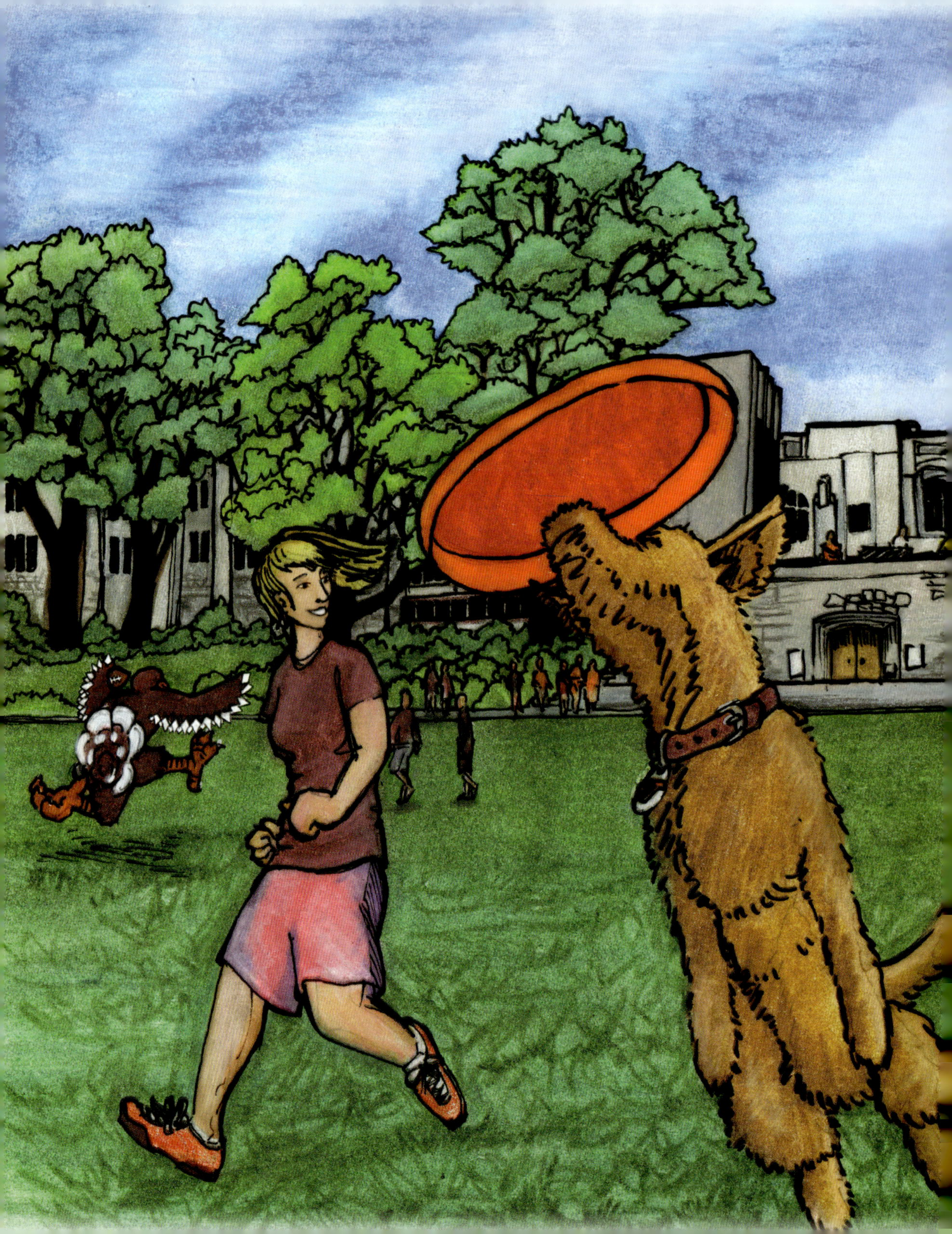

We played frisbee on the Drillfield, pick-up basketball at the War,
And skateboarded down the hallways—I mean, what is college for?

We slept through classes in McBryde, and studied late in Newman

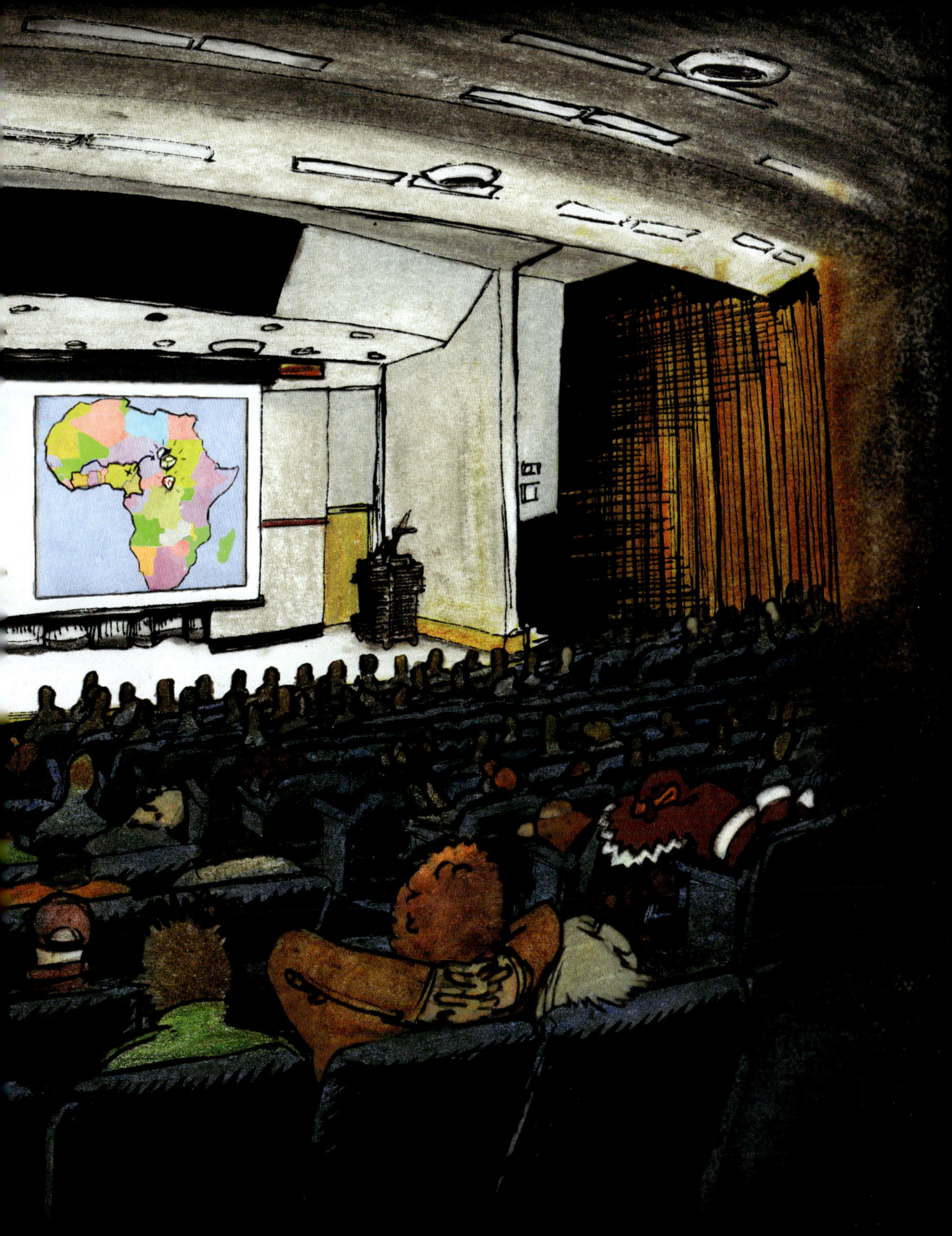

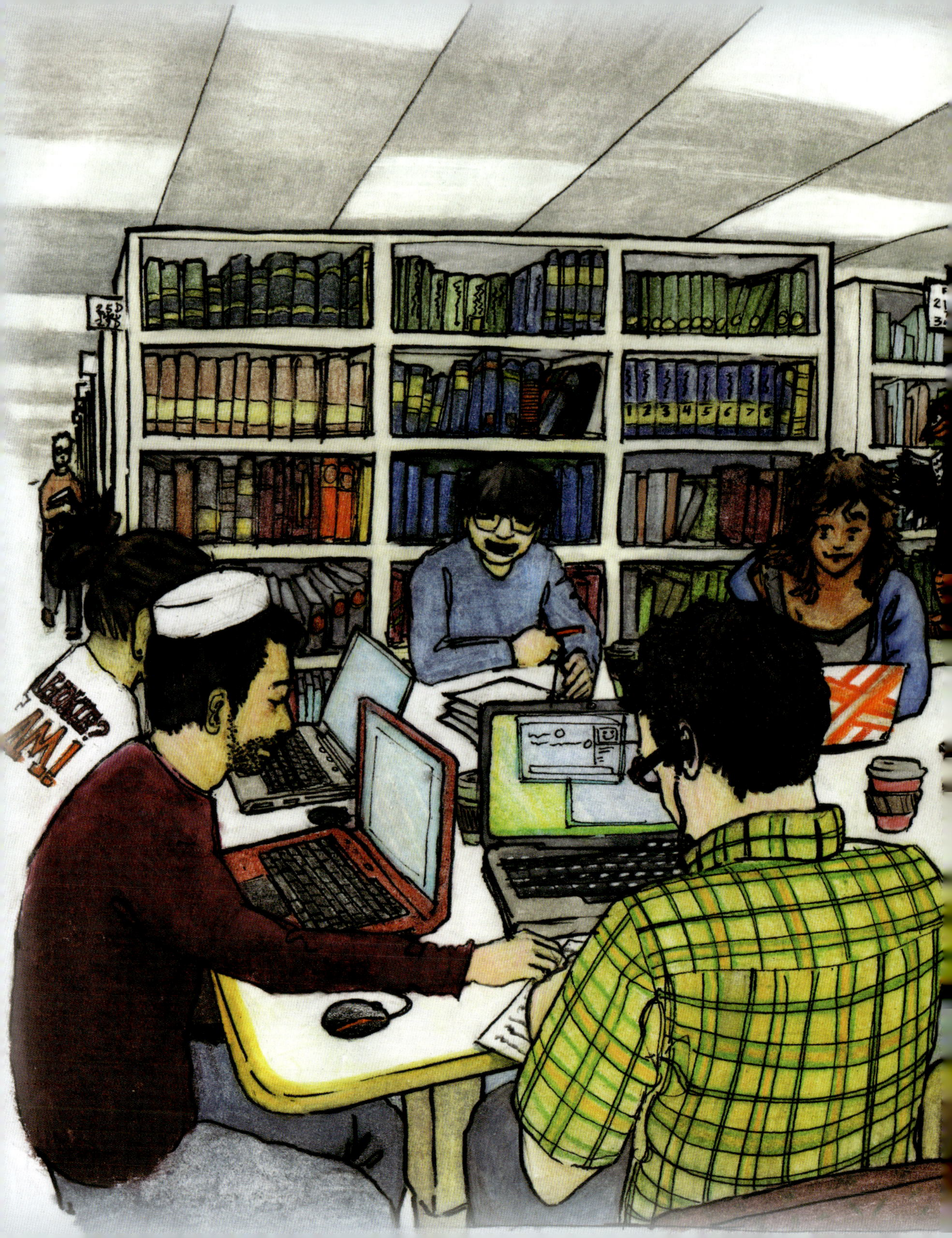
1 2 3 4 5 6 7 8
AM!

And in getting by on zero sleep, found new ways of being human.

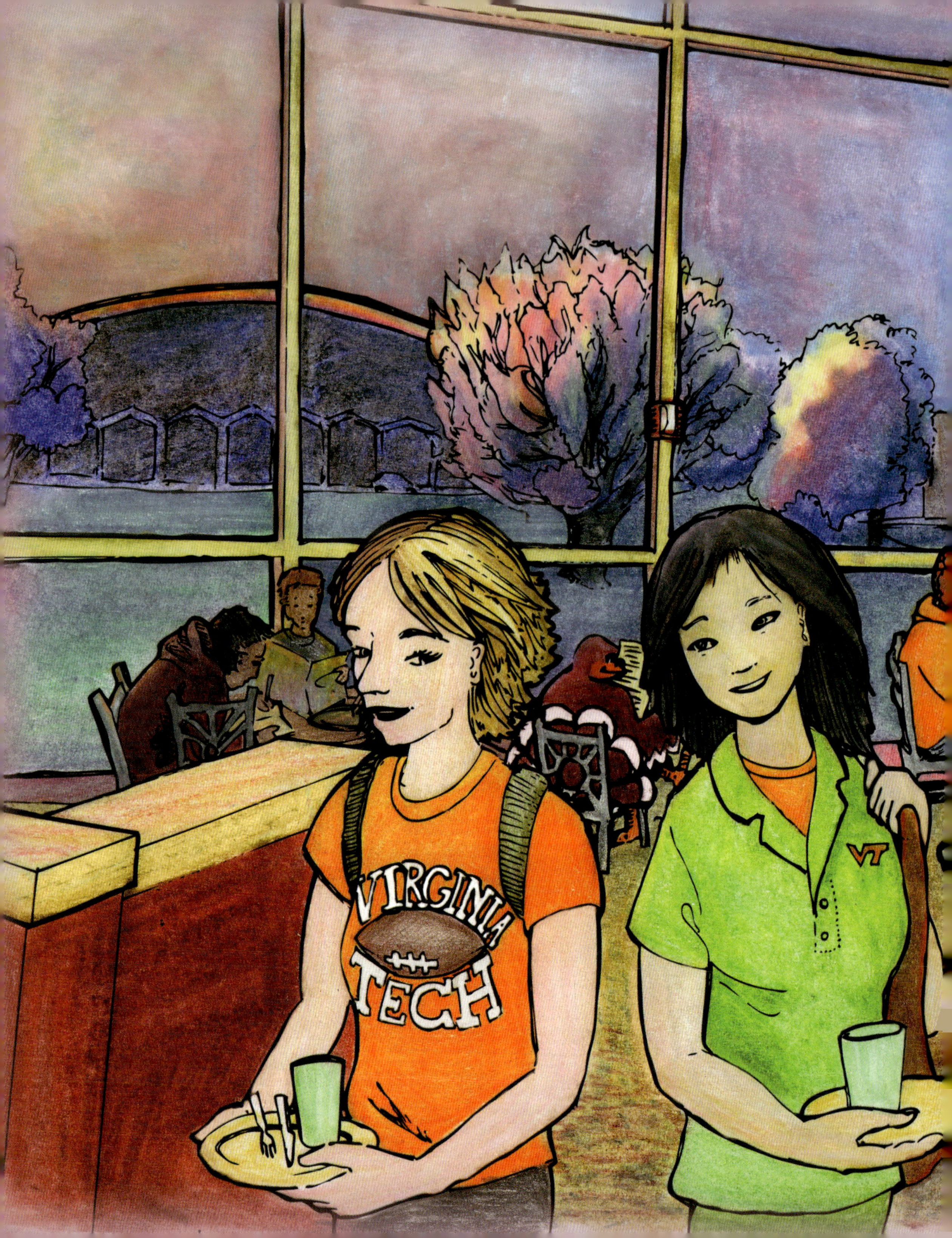
VIRGINIA
TECH
VT

We read CT upon waking up—our first "class" of the day—
We had to find out what the "He Said/She Said" kids would say!

And when we went to 8 o'clocks in PJs and little hoodies,
We carried KitKats in our pockets, and found there other funny goodies.

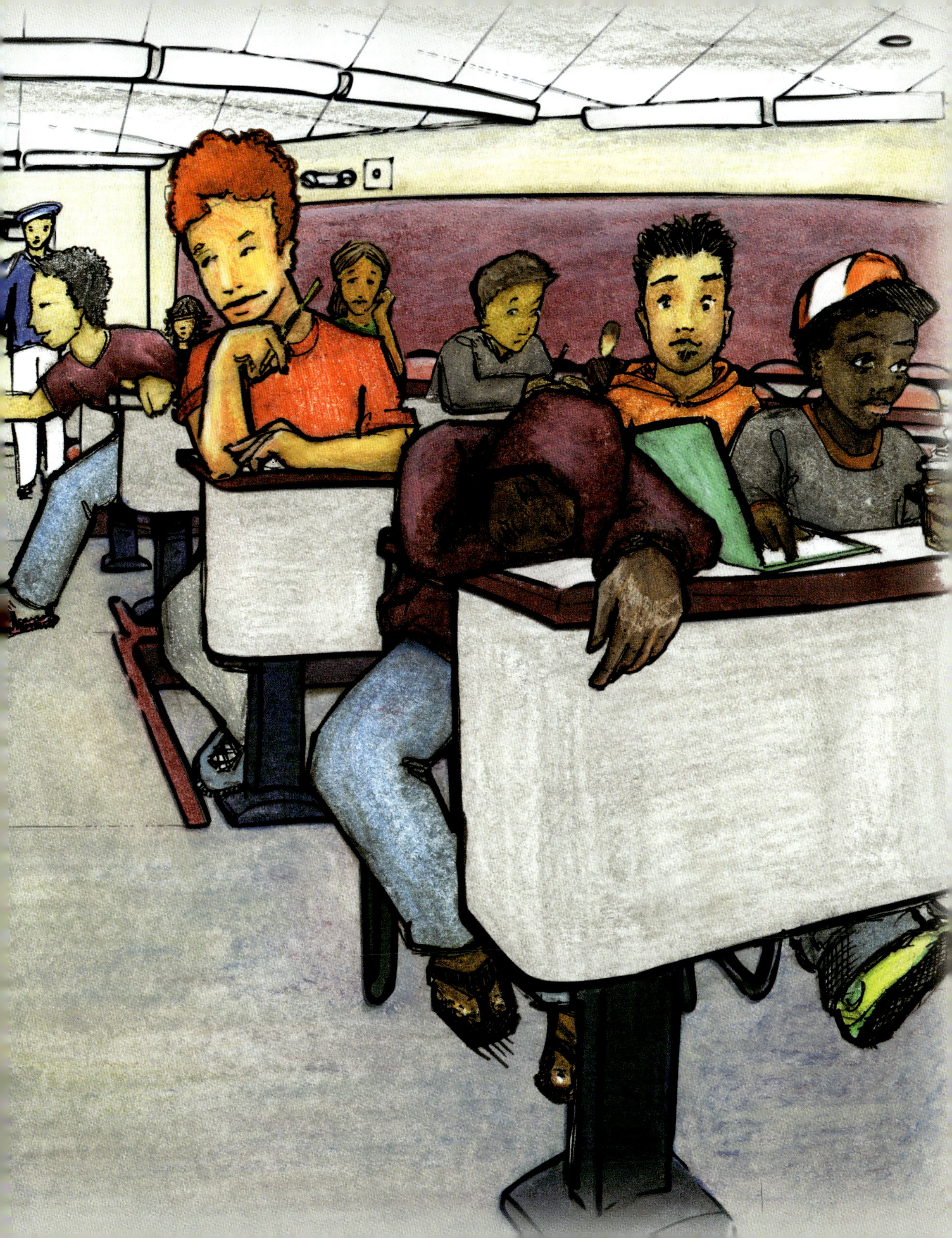

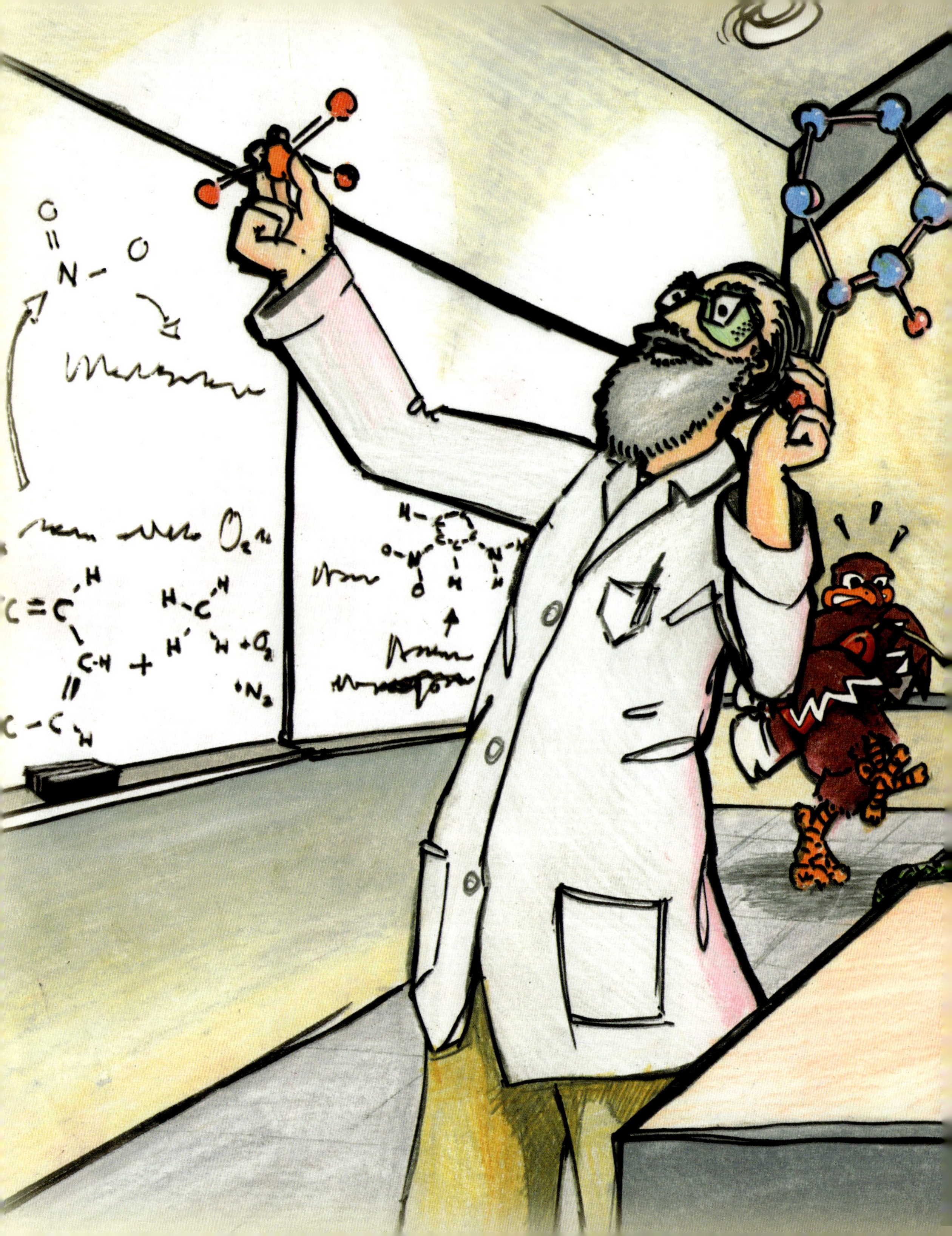

We learned from wise professors, who inspired us to think great thoughts,

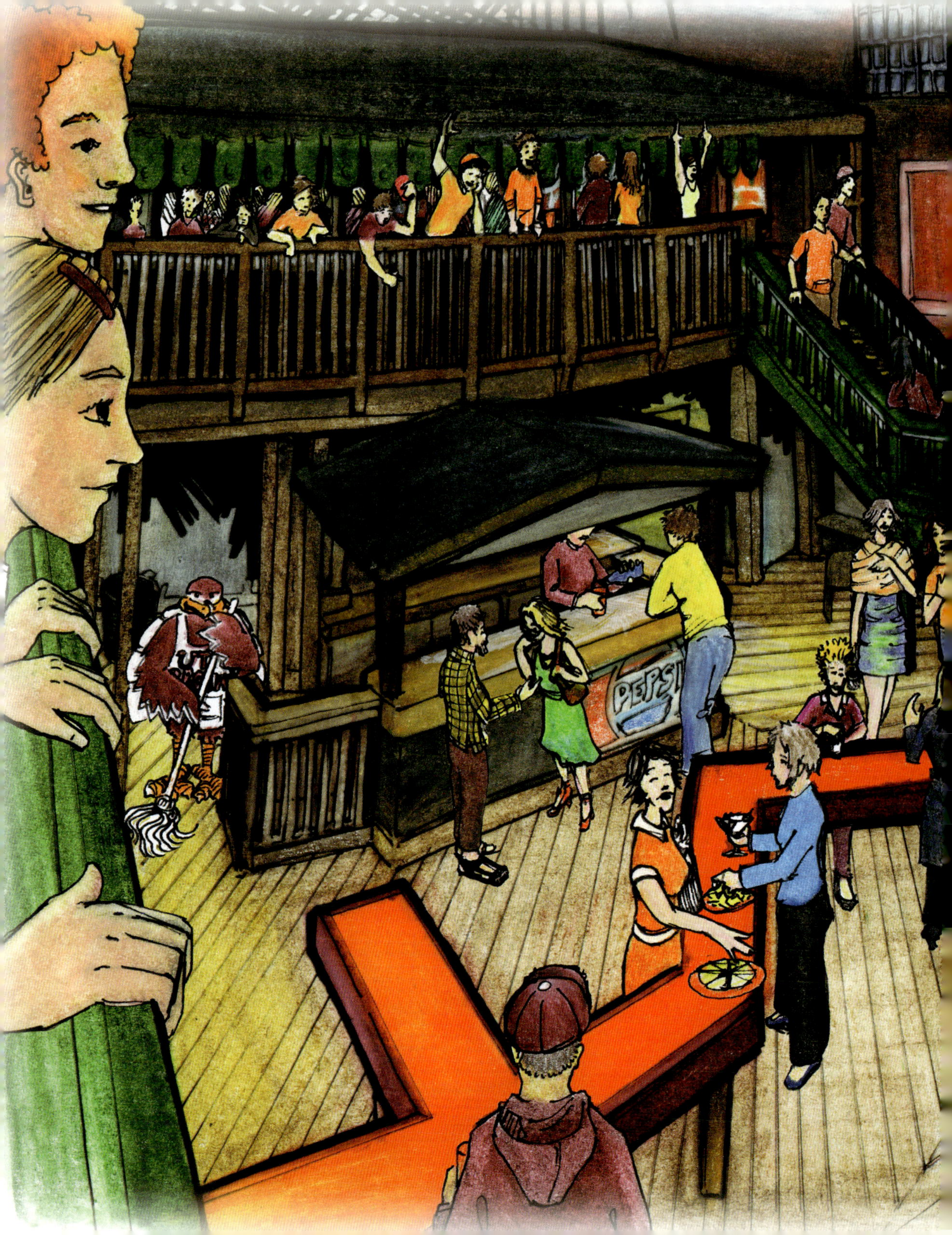
PEPSI

And then we had a wild time later on that night at TOTS.

We attended games at Lane in wild, adoring hordes
And loved to scorn our rivals, with their tomahawks and swords.

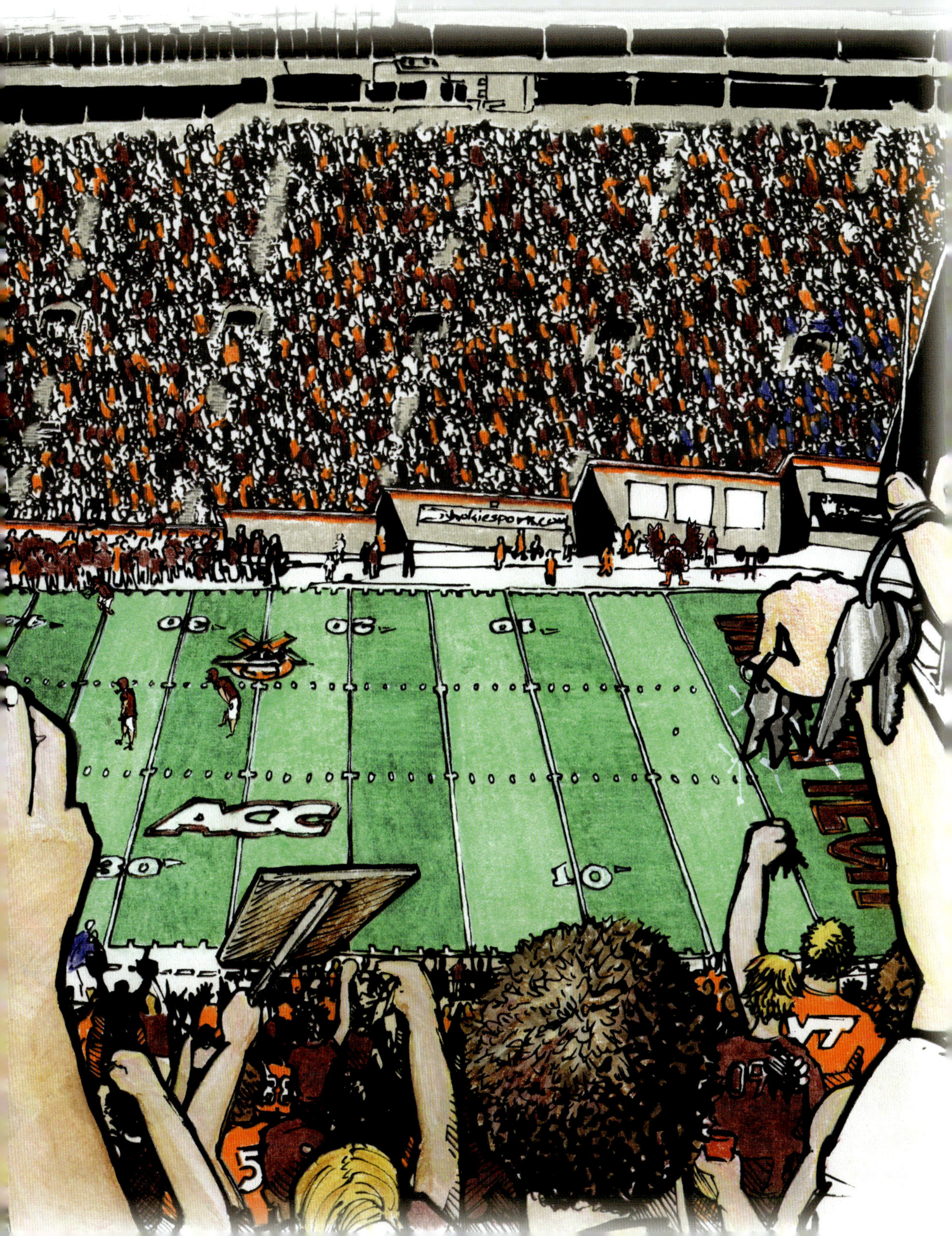
hokiesports.com
ACC
30
10
VT
5

We made out like savage lovers at the Duck Pond, don't you know,
Or anyway, we thought we did—can thinking make it so?

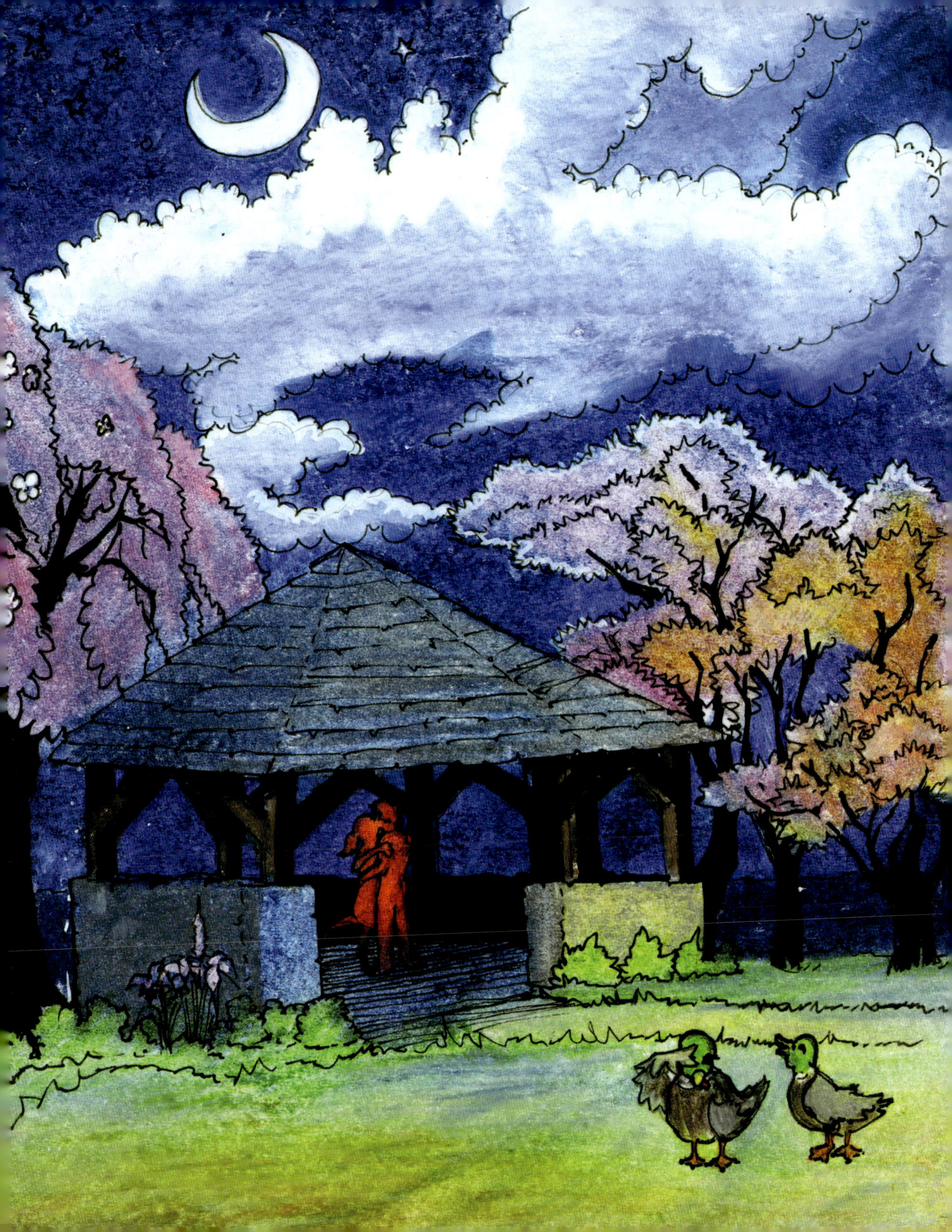

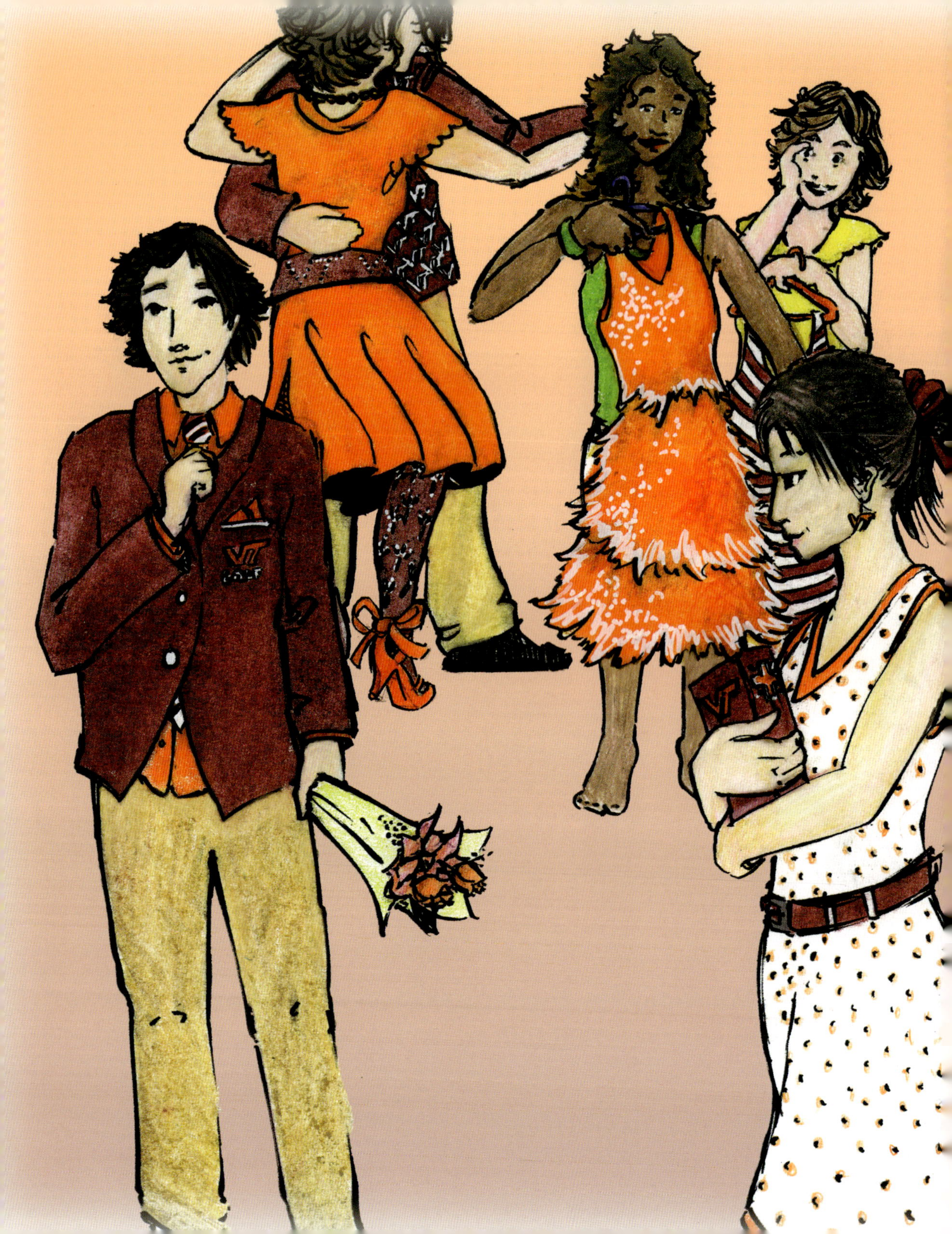

We wore maroon and orange to games, on dates, to church,
And whenever any wardrobe lack had left us in the lurch.

We danced the Hokie pokey in our sleep and for the cop;
Though he didn't think it funny, still, he didn't make us stop.

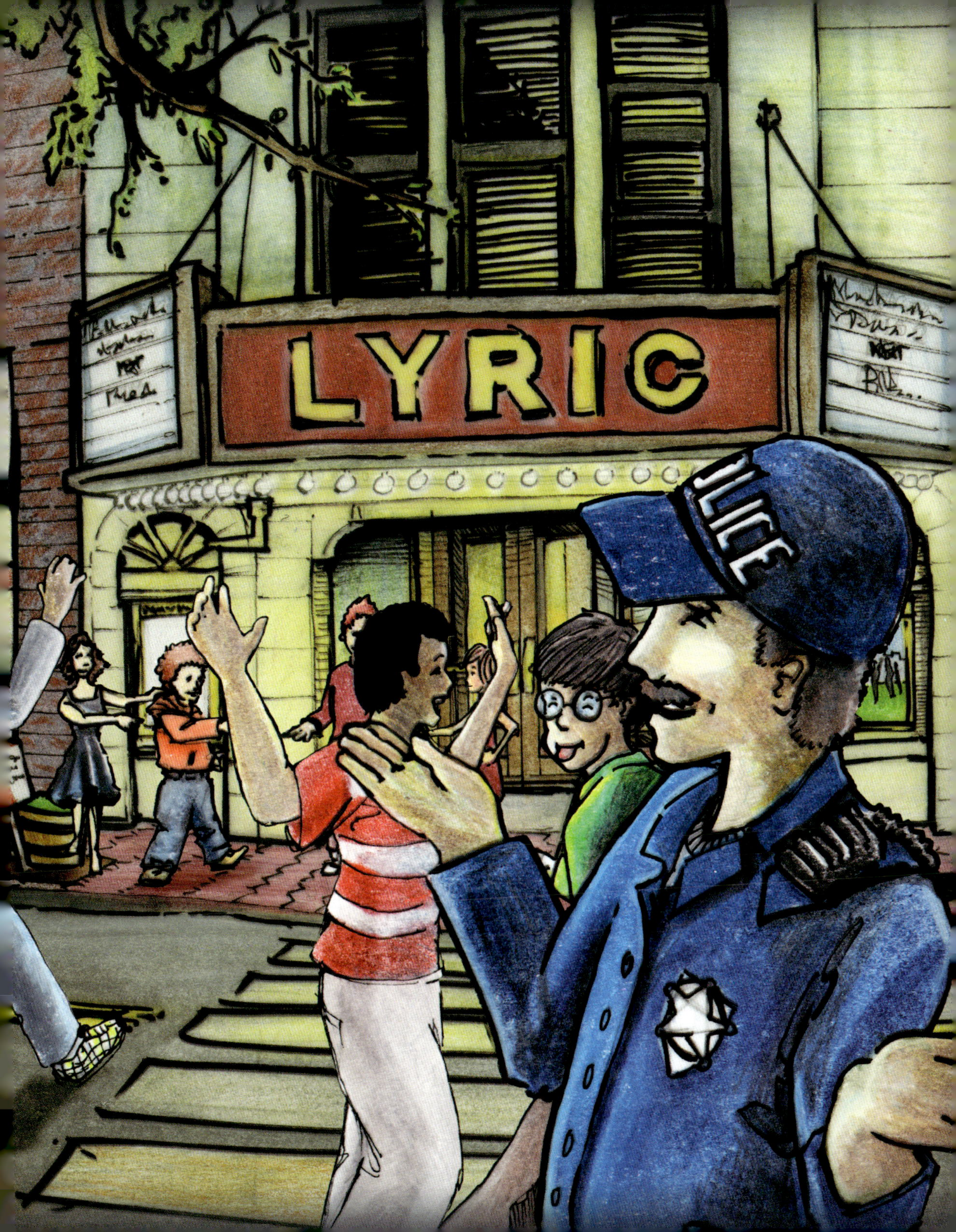
LYRIC

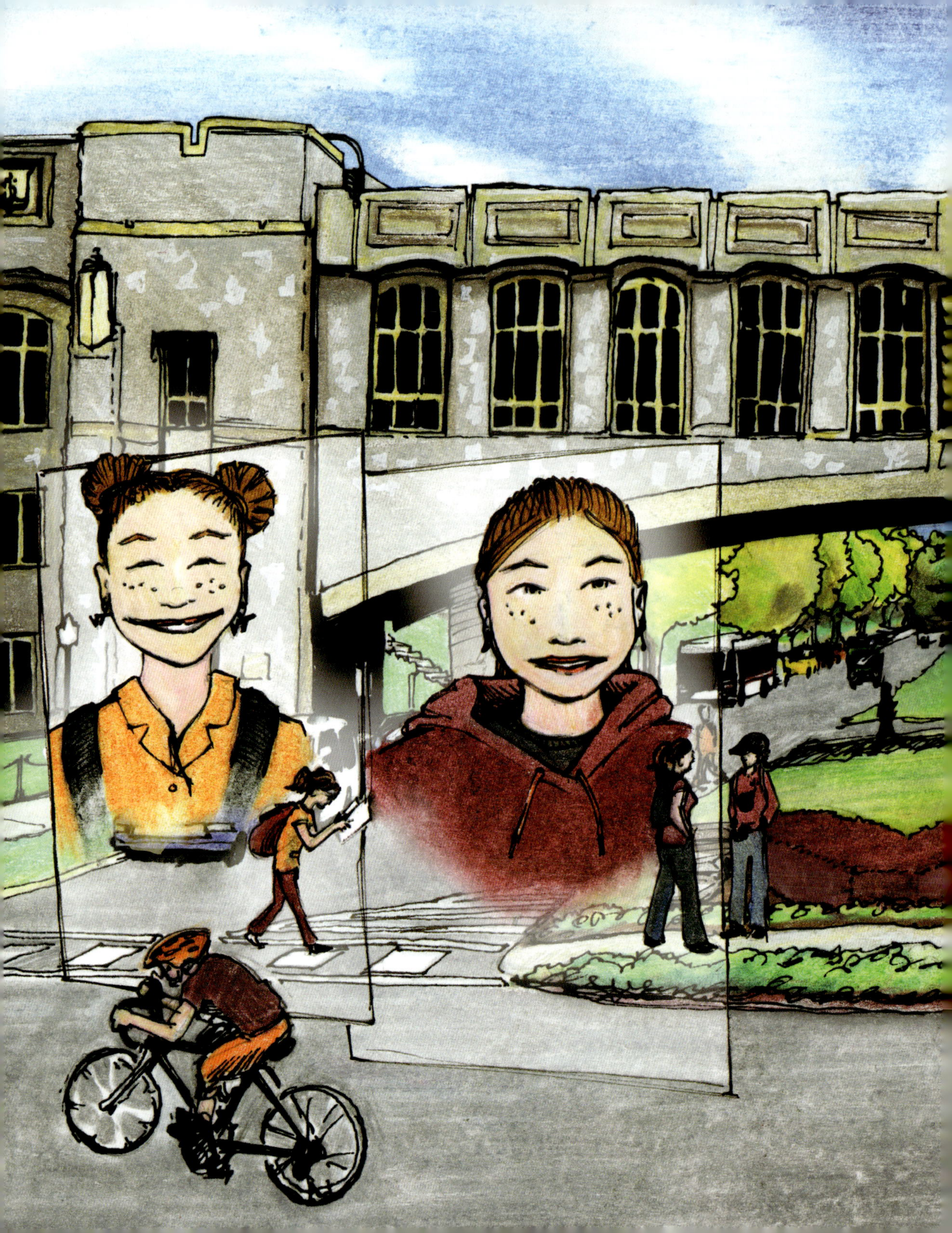

We took a risk and came here, not knowing how we'd grow,
And what effect this place would have on all that we now know.

Yes, you're a Hokie now, my friend. Tech gave you a fine start.

Whatever you become in life, you're a Hokie in your heart.

Key to Campus:
- ■ Academic Buildings
- ■ Administrative/Student Services
- ■ Athletics/Recreational Sports
- ■ Dining Facilities
- ■ Residence Halls
- ■ Town of Blacksburg

For the Uninitiated

the War	The War Memorial Gym
McBryde	building that has a big lecture hall, which many large classes are held in
Newman	the library
CT	Collegiate Times—the college newspaper
"He Said/She Said"	a column in the Collegiate Times
TOTS	Top Of The Stairs (TOTS), a popular watering hole in downtown Blacksburg, near campus
Lane	Lane Stadium—home of Hokie football!
tomahawks	the weapon of Florida State's mascot
swords	crossed swords—the emblem of the University of Virginia Cavaliers, arch rivals of the Hokies
maroon and orange	school colors